DATE DUE   AUG   2012

WEEKLY **WR** READER®
EARLY LEARNING LIBRARY

My Day at School

Going to School

by Joanne Mattern

Reading consultant: Susan Nations, M.Ed.,
author/literacy coach/
consultant in literacy development

Please visit our web site at: www.garethstevens.com
For a free color catalog describing Weekly Reader® Early Learning Library's list
of high-quality books, call 1-877-445-5824 (USA) or 1-800-387-3178 (Canada).
Weekly Reader® Early Learning Library's fax: (414) 336-0164.

Library of Congress Cataloging-in-Publication Data

Mattern, Joanne, 1963-
    Going to school / by Joanne Mattern.
      p. cm. — (My day at school)
    Includes bibliographical references and index.
    ISBN-10: 0-8368-6786-6 — ISBN-13: 978-0-8368-6786-2 (lib. bdg.)
    ISBN-10: 0-8368-6793-9 — ISBN-13: 978-0-8368-6793-0 (softcover)
    1. School children—Transportation—Juvenile literature.   2. School children—Juvenile literature.
    I. Title.
    LB2864.M35   2006
    371.8'72—dc22   2006005091

This edition first published in 2007 by
Weekly Reader® Early Learning Library
A Member of the WRC Media Family of Companies
330 West Olive Street, Suite 100
Milwaukee, WI 53212 USA

Copyright © 2007 by Weekly Reader® Early Learning Library

Editor: Barbara Kiely Miller
Art direction: Tammy West
Cover design and page layout: Kami Strunsee
Picture research: Diane Laska-Swanke
Photographer: Gregg Andersen

Printed in the United States of America

1 2 3 4 5 6 7 8 9 10 09 08 07 06

Note to Educators and Parents

Reading is such an exciting adventure for young children! They are beginning to integrate their oral language skills with written language. To encourage children along the path to early literacy, books must be colorful, engaging, and interesting; they should invite the young reader to explore both the print and the pictures.

The *My Day at School* series is designed to help young readers review the routines and rules of a school day, while learning new vocabulary and strengthening their reading comprehension. In simple, easy-to-read language, each book follows a child through part of a typical school day.

Each book is specially designed to support the young reader in the reading process. The familiar topics are appealing to young children and invite them to read — and re-read — again and again. The full-color photographs and enhanced text further support the student during the reading process.

In addition to serving as wonderful picture books in schools, libraries, homes, and other places where children learn to love reading, these books are specifically intended to be read within an instructional guided reading group. This small group setting allows beginning readers to work with a fluent adult model as they make meaning from the text. After children develop fluency with the text and content, the book can be read independently. Children and adults alike will find these books supportive, engaging, and fun!

— Susan Nations, M.Ed., author, literacy coach,
and consultant in literacy development

I walk to school. My dad
walks with me.

We are careful when we come to a **corner**. We look both ways before we cross the street.

I meet some friends on the way to school. They walk to school, too.

This corner has a **crossing guard**. She tells us when it is safe to cross the street.

This boy is riding a skateboard. What a fun way to go to school!

Some kids ride bikes to school. Dad says I can ride my bike to school when I am older.

Some moms and dads **drive** their children to school.

Lots of children ride the bus to school. They live too far away to walk.

There are many ways to get to school. But we all have to be here when the bell rings!

Glossary

corner — the place where two streets meet

crossing guard — a person who stops traffic and helps children cross a street safely

drive — to give someone a ride in a car; to work a car

skateboard — a short board with small wheels on the bottom, that a rider stands on. The rider rolls forward by pushing on the ground with one foot.

For More Information

Books

Crossing Guard. People in My Community (series). JoAnn Early Macken (Gareth Stevens)

My School Bus: A Book About School Bus Safety. My World (series). Heather L. Feldman (PowerKids Press)

Safety at School. Safety First (series). Joanne Mattern (Checkerboard Books)

Web Site

Back to School Safety Tips
www.nsc.org/mem/youth/8_school.htm
Learn how to get to school safely, whether you walk, ride a bike, take the bus, or ride in a car.

Publisher's note to educators and parents: Our editors have carefully reviewed this Web site to ensure that it is suitable for children. Many Web sites change frequently, however, and we cannot guarantee that a site's future contents will continue to meet our high standards of quality and educational value. Be advised that children should be closely supervised whenever they access the Internet.

Index

About the Author

Joanne Mattern has written more than one hundred and fifty books for children. Joanne also works in her local library. She lives in New York State with her husband, three daughters, and assorted pets. She enjoys animals, music, going to baseball games, reading, and visiting schools to talk about her books.